Miramichi

Tied by Marc Madore

Miramichi River

Gerry Williams holding a spring salmon caught on the Little Southwest Miramichi.

Miramichi River

Paul Marriner

Frank Amato
PORTLAND

River Journal

Volume 4, Number 4, 1996

About the Author

Paul and Nancy live on the South Shore of Nova Scotia near the small town of Mahone Bay and several Atlantic salmon rivers. A fly fisherman for thirty years, Paul has angled for Atlantic and Pacific salmon, trout, bass, and other fresh and salt water species in a dozen countries. He cast his first fly on the Miramichi and his attachment to this beautiful river has grown stronger with each passing season.

A member of the Outdoor Writers of Canada and the Outdoor Writers Association of America, Paul is the North American columnist for the Australian magazine *FlyLife,* a field editor for *Outdoors Canada,* and eastern Canadian correspondent for the Virtual Fly Shop. His articles have appeared in all major North American fly fishing, and a variety of outdoor, magazines, as well as a couple of overseas publications. Paul is the author of *Atlantic Salmon - A Fly Fishing Primer* (an Outdoor Writers award-winning book in 1994) and the *Ausable River Journal.* In 1991 Paul won the Gregory Clark Award for outstanding contributions to the arts of fly fishing.

◆

Acknowledgments

As always, it is impossible to acknowledge all of the people who have contributed in one way or another to my many enjoyable years of fishing, photographing, and writing about the Miramichi. However, special thanks are due the following: Cliff Brown, who introduced me to salmon fishing and the river; Bill Ensor of New Brunswick Tourism, without whose assistance this *River Journal* might not have been possible and for graciously consenting to read the manuscript (any errors are of course my own); Jerry Doak, who provided most of the flies; Bill Hooper, who offered valuable insights into the resource and its management and reviewed the applicable sections of this work; my brother Jim, absent whose prodding I would probably have spent many years fishing the same pool (and for too much else to record); Milton McKay, Gerry Williamson, and Brian Roadhouse, in whose company I have enjoyed many hours astream; Guy Smith, owner of Miramichi Gray Rapids Lodge, for several years of hospitality; Marc Madore, who developed and tied the signature pattern for this *River Journal*; Alex Mills and Vicki Oland-Mills, Keith and Linda Pond, Keith Wilson, Vin Swazey, "Hoot" Smith, Debbie Norton, George Holmes, Martin Budaker, and Flo Lyons, for their hospitality and assistance; Wayne Curtis, Don Nixon, Michael Augustine, Wes Myles, and Isobel Loughhead, for background help; the publishers of Gooselane Editions for research material; the Central New Brunswick Woodmen's Museum for permission to use material from William Griffin's, *You're on the Miramichi*; and finally, Frank Amato, for the opportunity to carry out this long anticipated project.

To Nancy, for her love, support and understanding.

◆

Series Editor: Frank Amato—Kim Koch

Subscriptions:
Softbound: $35.00 for one year (four issues)
$65.00 for two years
Hardbound Limited Editions: $95.00 one year, $170.00 for two years

Design: Alan Reid **Photography:** Paul Marriner (unless otherwise noted)
Fly plates by: Jim Schollmeyer
Map: Alan Reid
Softbound ISBN:1-57188-055-0, Hardbound ISBN:1-57188-056-9
(Hardbound Edition Limited to 350-500 Copies)

Miramichi River
New Brunswick, Canada

Author with fall salmon at the Miramichi Gray Rapids Lodge.

Miramichi River

◆

Introduction

"The world's greatest Atlantic salmon river," writes Wayne Curtis of the Miramichi River in *Currents in the Stream*. A sweeping statement, perhaps suspect by having been made by a native son. The evidence however supports the superlative. No other river sees as many angler days, produces as many Atlantic salmon, or offers such a length of fishable water.

According to Curtis, in his book, *Fishing the Miramichi*, the word Miramichi is a Montagnais (a native people of Quebec province) word for "Micmac land". The Micmacs (local aboriginal people) called the river Lust-a-gooch-cheech or Little Restigouche (another famous New Brunswick salmon river). Why the Montagnais word stuck, except perhaps that it was easier to pronounce and write, is a mystery.

Among the tens of thousands of anglers who have cast a fly over the Miramichi's storied waters are names from every field of endeavor. Writers, painters, musicians, educators, scientists, sports and movie stars, physicians, clergy, generals, business-men and -women, and politicians have made the journey, some many times. To all, the lure of the river and *Salmo salar* is irresistible.

I waded into the Miramichi for the first time over 25 years ago. The river's magic has drawn me back a hundred times since. The attachment is powerful. For almost 15 of those years my brother Jim owned a lodge on the river at Gray Rapids, now operated by Guy Smith as a commercial lodge, Gray Rapids Miramichi Lodge. Fortunately, Jim likes variety, and so we spent many hours tramping and casting over pools on all the tributaries.

I have never lived in the Miramichi valley, although for a time I lived in New Brunswick. So my viewpoint is necessarily that of a visitor, however frequent. Had this book been written by a resident, it would undoubtedly focus on different people, places and times.

Many great rivers are fully of the wilderness. Not so the Miramichi. Much of its lower valley has been inhabited for three centuries. The valley's people are as important to the river's story as the great silver fish which brought it angling fame. This *River Journal* celebrates all three.

Fish of the Miramichi

Atlantic Salmon

To fully appreciate the Miramichi, one must understand the fish which plays so large a part in the river's past, present and future. "In the beginning," Atlantic salmon eggs are laid in a gravel redd in November and hatch the next spring. The fry grow rapidly and within a few months acquire the characteristic bars and spots of a parr. One spring, after from two to three years in the river depending on the available food supply, the parr get a silver coat and a new name, smolt, and drop downriver to the ocean.

Now a genetic program (not yet fully understood) kicks in to protect the species from most natural disasters. Some smolts feed in the ocean for only one year and then return to the river. These are grilse, most weighing between three and six pounds. Some believe grilse are a subspecies and/or are all male. Both views are false, although the grilse population is significantly gender-biased in favor of males.

Salmon spending more than one winter at sea are called multi-sea-winter (MSW) fish. The number of years at sea determines the final size of a salmon returning home. Some think all large salmon have spawned several times—another myth. While an average of 30 percent of MSW salmon in the Miramichi spawn from two to four times, the majority are maidens. Most Miramichi spawners overwinter in the river and return to the sea in early spring. Called kelts, they feed primarily on an incoming run of spawning smelt.

Nowhere is a cliche more appropriate; Atlantic salmon don't put all their eggs in one basket. Should a catastrophe prevent spawning for several years, there are individuals returning for at least four years (in diminishing numbers to be sure) after their smolt run has left the river. And although their ocean survival rate is low, previous-year spawners often reenter the river after a few months of feeding in coastal waters, thus providing a defense against the loss of all year classes then at sea. Add to this: (1) a male parr can successfully fertilize a few eggs of a mature female, (2) salmon occasionally stray to other than their

Atlantic salmon holding. Photo by John Swedburg.

◆

natal rivers, and (3) salmon enter the river throughout the season; and one marvels at the intricate survival strategy of the species.

A famous Scottish salmon biologist once said, "Salmon don't feed in fresh water, but fortunately for you anglers they do take food." This is the final answer to an oft-debated question. If salmon didn't take food we couldn't catch them without nets or spears. But if salmon fed normally they would be found with full stomachs, which they are not-physiological changes that occur when they enter fresh water inhibit their ability to swallow. Regardless, most salmon anglers who fish frequently have seen the odd fish rising to a hatch of flies, its feeding instinct winning the battle with appetite suppression.

There is no historical evidence to suggest the Miramichi was ever home to very large salmon. Some argue the relative ease of migrating is responsible, but I am not persuaded. Other notable big fish rivers are no more difficult. Regardless, between 30 and 40 pounds seems a natural genetic limit. Due to conservation efforts, more salmon in this larger class are being landed and released each season.

Other Species

Atlantic salmon is the glamour species of the Miramichi, but it is not the sole inhabitant. While the lower river is too warm to support a large population of resident brook trout, it is a highway for anadromous brook trout headed for cold-water tributaries and the headwaters. This run peaks between mid-May and mid-June and trout over five pounds are taken each season.

Several tributaries were once famous for sea-trout runs. Twenty-five years ago, friends canoeing the Dungarvon in spring took extravagant numbers of trout. Likewise on the Cains. Sadly, this abuse contributed to the decimation of the runs. Although much well-deserved blame is heaped on anglers, forestry practices are equally responsible, particularly the myriad of forestry roads which reach every corner of the system. Brook trout are even more dependent than salmon on clean, cold-water brooks and removal of forest cover leads to both warming and siltation of these vulnerable waters.

"Sadly, we see no evidence of recovery," said noted New Brunswick fisheries biologist Bill Hooper when asked about the effectiveness of recent reductions in catch limits. Hooper attributes much of the problem to overfishing, lack of a size limit (preventing even one spawning cycle), and a widespread disrespect for the trout. The latter is a problem for any species sharing habitat with the 'king of gamefish'. "The only possible solution is the introduction of fly-fishing-only and catch-and-release regulations," said Hooper when asked for his recommendations.

Unlike salmon, anadromous brook trout feed. Thus they readily take bait and fly. Well upriver, where spring floods ebb earlier, lodges such as Governor's Table specialize in sea trout. The owner, "Hoot" Smith told me, "the trout arrive in schools starting in late May, so we can have great fishing one day but by the next the school has moved on. Then we have to find them again."

I rarely target brook trout on the lower Miramichi, neither salmon flies nor tackle being appropriate. But a few times 20 years ago, when salmon angling seemed hopeless, I downsized my fly and tippet and headed for a cold-water bogan (backwater fed by a brook or spring). The usual result was a half dozen or so plump brookies before they tired of the fly. And recently, while attempting to stir up some lethargic salmon at the mouth of a bogan by rapidly skating a large MacIntosh dry fly, I managed to irritate a sea-run of about 13 inches—the salmon naturally remained aloof.

Shad, another anadromous species, are virtually ignored by anglers. They enter the river in mid-May to spawn and are scarce by the end of June. One impediment to angling for them is the regulation banning weighted flies above the head of tide in the main river. Because shad rise poorly to a fly through the high spring water, most fishing is with fast-sinking lines. Regardless, those fishermen arriving properly equipped, and with a good variety of shad flies, can expect some excellent sport with little or no competition.

Striped bass are another sleeper species. While individuals have been seen as far upriver as Boisetown, most remain in the lower tidal regions of the main and Northwest rivers. "The stripers could provide excellent sport if their numbers weren't decimated by the by-catch in the gaspereaux [a small herring-like fish] and smelt nets," says Bill Hooper. An oft-delayed, no-retention regulation for the commercial fishery takes effect in 1996 so hopefully Bill's prediction will prove accurate.

"Striped bass populations were always thought to be cyclic, but we are now beginning to realize that it is probably commercial overfishing that has caused the perceived cycle," says Hooper. The bass enter the river in late fall to escape the decreasing saltwater temperatures and overwinter in the estuary. They spawn in early spring and then migrate to the ocean (they don't appear to travel far from the coast but spread widely). Presently they are caught mostly on lures, legal in the estuarine regions.

Geography

The Miramichi is actually a river system located in New Brunswick, one of Canada's east coast provinces. To be precise, which almost no one ever is, the Miramichi only exists for a few miles after its two main components, the Main Southwest Miramichi and the Northwest Miramichi, join near Miramichi City (formerly the towns of Newcastle and Chatham). From

◆

Angler poles past the camp of Dr. George Frederick Clarke (noted New Brunswick writer) near the Forks Pool, junction of North and South Branch of the Main Southwest Miramichi.

Shad in the evening.

◆

there the river flows to a rendezvous with Miramichi Bay and the Gulf of St. Lawrence. At its mouth it is nearly a mile wide. The first European to comprehend the full extent of the system was the young French engineer/cartographer, Batiste Louis Franquelin, who mapped the country in 1686. Regardless, most people speak of the Main Southwest as if it were the Miramichi and treat the Northwest as one of its tributaries, so I will follow this convention.

The Miramichi rises in the north central highlands of New Brunswick. On the way it gathers strength from six tributaries and scores of brooks and springs. Two of the six tributaries, the Taxis and Barnaby, are of no interest to salmon fishers. Both are small and see few, if any, salmon. However, the Renous and Northwest Miramichi have major tributaries of their own, the Dungarvon and the Little Southwest Miramichi respectively, all of which receive considerable salmon runs. The final two of the six, the Cains and Bartholomew, while both salmon streams, are also mismatched. The Cains is a major river while the Bartholomew is hardly larger than some well known brooks. Some also count the Bartibog as a tributary, but it flows into the estuary so close to Miramichi Bay that most don't consider it part of the system.

The Main Southwest Miramichi

Near the tiny town of Juniper, the North and South Branches of the Main Southwest Miramichi River coalesce at the Forks Pool. Here, from the porch of his camp, George Frederick Clarke, dentist and author, watched the waters mix and the salmon leap, or excavated aboriginal campsites beneath his feet. In the dining room of nearby Governor's Table Lodge, owner "Hoot" Smith told me, "The Forks Pool has changed a lot since old Clarke's time. The North Branch keeps cutting a new channel, moving the pool farther and farther downstream."

The branches spring from a series of cold-water brooks. They are not, however, equal in importance when considering spawning areas for salmon and sea-run brook trout. The North Branch receives the majority of fish and so historically was

Poling through a "Louie" on the Main Southwest Miramichi

most important from an angling perspective (access is currently restricted by the corporate owner of the surrounding forest land).

Between the forks and Boisetown (about 50 miles) the character of the river changes frequently. After some 35 miles of rapids, runs, and pools, a dozen miles of essentially riffle water begins.

As he picked a canoe route with pole and paddle through one of the many shallow riffles between Rocky Brook and Ludlow, Larry Seymour, a guide at Pond's Resort, suggested, "There isn't a lot of fishing in this stretch except at a few good pools." Courtesy of Keith Pond, Larry was giving me my first glimpse of this section of the river. While he worked, I thought

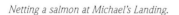

Netting a salmon at Michael's Landing.

of the millions of parr such insect factories nourish each year.

Although far from a sharp dividing line, downstream of Boisetown the river begins to braid extensively. Here the bottom is primarily gravel and annually islands and bars resist or succumb to the awesome power of the spring ice. Once-productive pools fill in and new holding water is created in previously indifferent locations. A favorite pool of my early salmon fishing days, Michael's Landing, simply disappeared one year when the spring ice carried away the gravel bar which gave it shape. Fortunately, it now appears the river has begun a restoration.

The mouth of the Cains marks another change in the river's appearance. Downstream there are fewer gravel bars (and only one island), more long runs and heavy rapids, and a bottom of larger stones. Finally, a few miles beyond the foot of White Rapids, is the bridge at Quarryville. This is the head of tide and some 30 miles from the mouth of the river. Here, as well, the Renous pushes over a major gravel bar to join the Main Southwest.

Quarryville also marks the end of salmon angling on the main river. Below the bridge the gradient diminishes and the flow is slow and deep. Although some might quibble over this, Quarryville is the most heavily fished pool on the river. On some days I have counted over 60 anglers there, casting from anchored boats, working both sides of the river from shore, or covering the mouth of the Renous.

With few exceptions, all the rivers in the system are cut from the same cloth. The pattern depends on the gradient and the nature of the surrounding land. In the headwaters, big gradients produce pothole country, where small pools filled with jumbled rocks predominate. Moderate gradients are marked by sand and gravel spaces between stones but are still punctuated

10

by the odd large boulder. Here and there, geologic thrusts yield attractive ledge pools. The low gradient sections, referred to as steadies, are surrounded by alder scrub and have soft organic bottoms. As stream size increases, one finds more riffles and runs ending in classic pools with gravel, rock, or ledge rock bottoms.

Geography aside, most anglers worry over the amount of open water, that is, public fishing. Compared to the Main Southwest, with only about 10 percent of its length freely available to the public, several of the tributaries are almost entirely open water. Regardless, the Miramichi is like few other salmon rivers in that many, many, miles of the private water on the Main Southwest are available to the public by the simple expedient of picking up the phone and making a reservation with one of the commercial lodges.

History of the River

The wonder is that there are any Atlantic salmon in the Miramichi today. When Europeans first arrived at the mouth of the river over 350 years ago, one wrote, *So large a quantity of them [salmon] enters into this river that at night one is unable to sleep, so great is the noise they make in falling upon the water after having thrown or darted themselves into the air.* Though few in number, the colonists set about with considerable ingenuity and gusto to bring silence to the night.

The chosen weapons were nets and spears. Set nets ringed the bay and stretched across the river, pools were swept with nets by day and night, and canoes set out for the spawning grounds after dark bearing flambeaux (torches) and spears. So prodigious was the slaughter that by 1789 almost a million and a half pounds of salmon were exported from the Miramichi. A good night for the upriver spearers could see 1000 carcasses hauled ashore. The celebrated storyteller, George F. Clarke, tells of his grandfather spearing 50 salmon in 1838 during the short float from Blackville to White Rapids.

The vast depredations soon took their toll and the salmon runs declined precipitously. Combined with the rapid development of a more lucrative forestry industry, the collapse caused the commercial operations to virtually evaporate. The remaining salmon were hardly left in peace. Netting and spearing for local consumption and the negative impacts of mills and log drives continued to take a toll.

The latter half of the 19th century saw the first effective regulation of the salmon fishery and the establishment of fish culture stations. Undoubtedly this saved the Miramichi's salmon from the ultimate fate of those in other rivers. Regardless, the original runs—estimated at a million fish— would never be seen again.

Apparently, few sportsmen ventured to the Miramichi before the mid-1800s. Certainly the local people were little interested in sport, concerned as they were with wrestling a living from the valley and considering the ease with which salmon could be taken with net and spear. After 1850, angler/authors tell of fly fishing the Miramichi and having some success. Charles Hallock wrote in 1873 that the favored areas were well upstream of the nets, around the mouths of cold-water brooks such as Rocky, Burnt Hill, Salmon, and Clearwater Brooks on the main river. Others favored wilderness tributaries such as the Sevogle.

While some travellers reported acceptable angling, others suggested the river was so netted and poached as to be useless

Salmon leaping beside anglers at the Miramichi Gray Rapids Lodge.

Bill Ensor at the Forks Pool, the junction of North and South Branches of the Main Southwest Miramichi.

◆

for sport. Regardless, from this time forward, fly fishing for Atlantic salmon on the Miramichi increased in popularity. Although mentions of the earliest commercial lodges are very scarce in the surviving literature, angler/writers such as F.G. Aflalo were running the river at the turn of the century. They engaged guides and camped at many of the same spots we would today.

One early commercial operation was Murdock McKenzie's lodge near The Forks (juncture of the North and South Branch

◆

River canoe on the North Branch, Main Southwest Miramichi.

of the main river). "McKenzie would pick up sports from the U.S. in Bristol and drive them to the camp," said Don Nixon. Ninety years young, Don still lays out a line for salmon, although he retired from guiding a few years back. "Then the sports and guides would head downriver in dugouts for the trip to Boisetown," Don explained. The usual trip lasted from a week to 10 days.

The wilderness experience must have been more important than the fishing for, as Don pointed out, "you didn't have to go very far to catch salmon, the pools were full of them." After the trip the sports would return home from Boisetown and the guides would pole the canoes back to McKenzie's in two days.

Don did not hesitate when asked to compare the dugouts of those days to the modern canoe. "The dugout was better than anything you'll find today," he said. "Turney Grey, from up the North Branch, made some great ones. He would go into the woods and find a suitable pine, rough shape it on the spot and then pull it out to his place to finish. They were 30-foot long and would make six to seven miles an hour going upriver. When you gave them a push they just kept on gliding."

The dugouts had mostly disappeared from the river by 1930, in part because the skill of the builders was not being passed on, but also because suitable trees were getting harder to find. The replacements were lapstrake or canvas canoes. An example of an early dugout can be seen at the Woodmen's Museum in Boisetown. However, Don Nixon explained, "it's not a particularly good one, much heavier than the best of the early models."

One other development significantly affected early salmon angling on the Miramichi, the formation of fishing clubs. As far back as the last decades of the 19th century, stretches of government-owned riverbank have been leased to individuals or groups (this is in addition to the exclusive fishing rights associated with the ownership of land in certain original grant areas). Shares were sold in these clubs, mostly to wealthy anglers from the northeastern United States. One well known example is The Miramichi Fish and Game Club which came into existence on the Northwest Miramichi in 1893 (although anglers had been plying the "club" waters for two decades previously). Edward Weeks wrote a history of the club in 1984 featuring a riveting photo of a 36-pound monster taken by William Crawford in 1893.

A few enterprising, turn-of-the-century anglers also headed to the upper Miramichi for trout. Tappan Adney recorded a 1902 excursion by canoe up the North Branch for native and sea-run brook trout. Adney describes the Alder Ground in the same way as I would after seeing the area in 1995. The group had superb fishing although Adney was a little disappointed in not catching one of the seven- to eight-pound monsters reputed to be in the stream (the largest they landed was three and one half pounds).

People of the Miramichi

The original inhabitants of the Miramichi valley were Micmacs. Today, as it was 3000 years ago, the native peoples are clustered in two areas, Redbank, at the confluence of the Northwest and Little Southwest Rivers and Eel Ground on the Northwest. "Redbank is recognized as New Brunswick's oldest community," said Michael Augustine, a Redbank Band councillor.

Michael also broadened my knowledge of fish species in the Miramichi. "Two thousand years ago sturgeon was a major food fish for our people." When I suggested that the fish was long gone, he disagreed, "Very scarce, it's true, but several years ago when we were still gill-netting, a six-foot, 120-pound sturgeon was caught in a gill net and released after several hours of examination. We were amazed when it swam away unharmed."

The bands still operate food fisheries but the gill nets have been replaced by trap nets. "In addition to respecting quotas for salmon and grilse, we also collect information on the runs for the DFO [Federal Department of Fisheries and Oceans]," Michael said. The people of Redbank have also been involved in the sportfishery for 75 years, mostly providing guide services. Today, however, there is also a commercial lodge operated by Wilfred Ward, Broken Feather Lodge, situated in the community.

The ultimate European settlers of the valley were mostly Irish and Scottish, and it was said that they got tougher the farther up the river one went. The region brooked little weakness, and many died from the harsh realities of woods and river work. To this day, either one is born on the Miramichi or is "from away", and living there for a score of years will not change your status. Regardless, even strangers get a friendly wave as they drive the roads.

On the Miramichi for generations, many wilderness-hardened, resourceful people have been in daily, albeit seasonal, contact with folks whose material wealth vastly exceeds their own. Has this affected their character? Certainly. In most it produces a healthy irreverence for the trappings of affluence

Black Brook Salmon Club on the Cains River. Photo by Jim Marriner.

Brian Roadhouse with a salmon at the Miramichi Gray Rapids Lodge.

◆

and, to be sure, the foibles of some self-absorbed visitors are often fodder for a cracklin' good winter story.

The region has produced more than its share of writers, musicians, artists, poets, and songwriters. Three of the best known contemporary writers are the brothers Wayne and Herb Curtis and David Richards (an award winning novelist). "I think the best way to characterize the difference between my writing and Herb's is that I strive for drama, Herb for humour," says Wayne Curtis. Wayne has written several books of fiction and non-fiction set in the valley, his latest is *Fishing the Miramichi*.

Herb Curtis tells his stories through the lives of his characters Shadrack and Dryfly, two young men from the valley of the Dungarvon River. The trilogy, *The Americans are Coming*, *The Last Tasmanian*, and *The Lone Angler*, follow Shadrack and Dryfly as they pass through their teens in the late sixties and early seventies. Although Herb draws much humour from the lives and peculiarities of his Dungarvon characters, there is an equal portion of the mysticism and pathos inherent in their isolated existence with its but quicksilver connection to the wider world.

Of course, in the space available, it is impossible to recognize the scores of poets and songwriters of the Miramichi whose work will never travel far from the region. Fortunately, much has been preserved; sadly, the oral tradition, as it has in many cultures, is disappearing beneath the pervasive cloak of modern communications. All the same, famous ballads such as

"The Dungarvon Whooper", written by the celebrated valley poet Michael Whelan (1858-1937) about a legendary lumber camp murder, are still sung along the river.

Tactics for Atlantic Salmon

A *River Journal* offers insufficient space to exhaustively describe, with examples, the techniques of fly fishing for Atlantic salmon. Several books on the subject are currently available (including my own, *Atlantic Salmon: A Fly Fishing Primer*). Thus, what follows is a brief summary of my approach (others may view things differently). Additional material will be found in the chapters about the seasons.

Salmon fishing can be divided into three situations; 1) covering the water, 2) fishing for a discovered salmon, or 3) trying for a visible fish. Number one often leads to number two. In all situations the angler has the choice of wet, damp, or dry-fly techniques.

"Covering the water" is a methodical approach to presenting a fly to all possible salmon lies in a pool. The standard, or "classic", technique is to cast a wet fly down-and-across, adjusting the angle with current velocity to swim the fly at an attractive speed (learned from streamside instruction or experience). Except in early spring and occasionally in the fall, a floating line is usually appropriate as Atlantic salmon will rise to a fly providing the water is not too cold. A damp, or waking, fly may replace the wet fly, or a standard wet pattern may be riffled across the surface by having the leader emerge from the side of the head (a riffling, or Portland hitch).

Adjusting your casting angle will not yield the desired fly speed, adjustments are made by stripping line during the swing or mending. Also, some twitch the swimming fly by moving the rod tip. I do this mostly with split wing flies.

Covering the water with a dry fly is more laborious, but still popular when the water warms sufficiently (usually above 50 degrees). The approach is up-and-across, extending the drift with mends and feeding line. To limit casting, one selects the best looking current lanes, paying particular attention to seams.

While covering the water produces plenty of salmon, the angler (and/or guide) must pay close attention to the fly. Often salmon rise to a fly without touching it, the only indication being a slight disturbance of the surface or even just a subsurface flash. This is an interested, or discovered, salmon. How long you can spend with a discovered salmon depends on whether or not you are alone. First, rest the salmon for a moment and then show it the same fly, cast in exactly the same way. Should that fail, change the speed of the fly, then the size of the pattern (and/or tippet size), and finally the pattern itself. After all that, if you have the patience, see if some response can be elicited with the variety of wet, dry, and damp techniques described below for addressing a visible fish. I would never, however, leave a discovered salmon without one final repetition of the original fly and cast.

Wet fly tactics for a visible salmon are varied (again assuming you have the pool to yourself!). Attempt multiple approach angles and speeds. Later, try sinking leaders (or sink-tip lines) to alter fly depth or upstream nymph techniques where water depths are suitable. Dry fly tactics include; dead drift, pulling

Quarryville Pool.

the fly several times over the salmon's head followed by a dead drift, or twitching the fly. All are accompanied by multiple fly changes involving size, color, and style. Clearly a vast number of possibilities exist. If the salmon responds to a particular approach, concentrate on that with changes in flies. Should there be no interest whatsoever within a half-hour, I would move on and return later when the light has changed.

The preceding is, condensed to a fare-thee-well, how to fish for Atlantic salmon. Unexplored are a wide variety of opinions about the order of changes in approaches and flies, how long one should persist (to rest or not to rest), at what speeds various flies should be fished, which flies and sizes work best in specific conditions of water temperature and height, how light affects choice of fly and approach, etc.

Fall fishing at Kelly's Channel.

Floating a bomber (dry fly fishing).

◆

Although it occurred on the Harry's River in Newfoundland, I can't resist an illustrative personal experience. The pool was mine alone (public but unoccupied). A fish of some 12 pounds rose to, but did not touch, my fly. Seven more times that salmon teased me, each time on the initial cast of a new wet pattern, providing the presentation was identical to the first. No other approach (damp or dry, faster or slower, sinking leader, etc.) elicited the slightest response. After almost two and a half hours, with a tricky wade across the river in the gathering darkness looming, I surrendered. Such is Atlantic salmon fishing.

Tributary Experiences

Cains River

The Cains River melds with the main river a few miles upstream of the town of Blackville. Fed by boggy upriver springs, its waters acquire a characteristic dark stain. Although the once renowned spring sea-trout run is in trouble, it remains an attractive stream with an excellent fall run of salmon and is beloved by many hunters for its grouse and woodcock covers.

Under a cobalt sky, Buttermilk Brook Pool is breathtakingly beautiful in an understated, wilderness way. During a recent visit under low water conditions with John Huff and Brian Roadhouse, two frequent angling companions, I was fortunate to land one grilse and release another fishing the outside of the bend. But John, with years of experience on Quebec salmon rivers, sensed the other side of the river would be more productive. And it was, as he quickly raised several fish, hooked and lost a salmon, and then landed and released a pretty female of 10 pounds on a size 12 Chartreuse Muddler.

A visit to the Cains is never amiss. Many of the pools remind one of flowing dark ale topped with streaks of foam. Even the quintessential Cains fly, the Copper Killer, reflects this coloration with its "stained" body of copper tinsel. Jim has canoed the river twice (I have yet to make the float) and speaks eloquently of the special character of the journey. Next year it's my turn.

Bartholomew River

I have little first-hand experience of the Bartholomew as a salmon stream. The reason being that until recently it was designated an "index river" (reserved for scientific study) and so closed to salmon angling. Studies record the run size as varying

◆

John Huff tails a salmon on the Cains River.

wildly from year to year (under 200 to over 2000), and in some years it seems most salmon arrive after the season closes. Bill Hooper notes, 'the salmon remain in two deep water pools about a mile above the counting station throughout the summer and early fall. Up-river migration begins only after the second week of October several days before spawning.'

Dungarvon River

Sharing a friend's first salmon is a satisfying experience. Several years back I took Brian Roadhouse, an accomplished trout and steelhead fisher, and Liz Wylie, to M & M Whooper Hollow Lodge on the Dungarvon River. Brian needed but a few hours to hook and land his first salmon—an event surrounded by much encouragement and coaching. Just to prove the result was no fluke, he plucked a grilse from the river the next morning. However, this ended our fishing, for a torrential rain began that afternoon. After three days the river had risen four feet (I have the photos to prove it). At one point we thought our trip would be extended when the river summarily annexed the road.

Under normal conditions the Dungarvon should be approached with small river techniques. By this I mean that movement is essential. Rather than cast over one or two pools extensively, the angler should cover as many as possible. Steelheaders will understand perfectly. Dan Fowler, a friend who cherishes the Dungarvon, commented during an excursion, "When the main river is too warm for the salmon to be active, I can often track down a fish or two in the cooler waters here."

Renous River

Jim and I have stalked the Renous River many times through the years. Nonetheless, it has seldom been kind to me. I have previously told of instructive experiences with a Bomber and oddball classic salmon flies in my book, *Atlantic Salmon: A Fly Fishing Primer*, and magazine articles. Regardless, the

◆

Brian Roadhouse fights salmon on the Dungarvon River.

Black Brook Salmon Club on the Cains River.

◆

Renous experience which comes to mind each time I hear the name is a visit to The Rock Ponds.

The Rock Ponds are aptly named. They are rocky stillwaters in which salmon pause while ascending the North Branch of the river. Depending on conditions, the angling can be excellent. Jim, Gerry Williamson, and I, began the long walk in on a day when the air was heavy with humidity and as still as in the burial chamber of King Tut's tomb—perfect conditions for no-see-ums. These minute menaces breach all defenses. No mesh is small enough, and only the foolish put insect repellent on their eyelids.

The flies from hell attacked as soon as we arrived. Like demons with brimstone tipped tridents, they closed in on the eyes, nostrils, lips, and ears. It seemed as if the salmon, showing frequently near the inlet to the pond, were enjoying our discomfort. After an hour of misery without a touch, we capitulated.

Although having happily wandered up the North Branch of the Renous casting Bugs over rock-studded pothole pools, I prefer the gravel bottom and classic pools of the middle river. At normal water levels one can cross back and forth to approach each pool from the proper side. And, once again, movement is important in this section as most pools are small and unlikely to hold more than one or two fish.

Little Southwest Miramichi River

Murry's Landing on the Little Southwest, about a half-mile above Andre Godin's Miramichi Inn, is a favorite summer pool. On a sunny, but crisp, April day, in the company of my brother Jim and good friend Milton McKay, it also yielded my first spring salmon while fishing from shore. Casting from huge chunks of ice thrown up on shore by the spring flood, it was fascinating to watch the salmon rise for our easily visible, bright colored streamers. This is unusual for the Miramichi as angling is almost always at water level (canoe or wading). The experience reminded me of fishing from platforms in Norway.

I am inured to the assault on my ego when a nearby novice hooks a big salmon with an inept spaghetti cast and then lands

Elizabeth Wylie fall fishing on the Dungarvon.

◆

it after making every possible error. But when I am shown up by an experienced angler, the cut bleeds deeply. Late one morning, while fishing the home pool of Upper Oxbow Angling Adventures' lodge, I rose a salmon. After several fly, speed, and approach angle changes, I moved on. A stranger, who had been sitting patiently on a streamside log, arose, stepped in behind me and hooked and landed "my" fish. To add to my pain, as he followed me through the pool, he hooked two more salmon. Luckily for me he was a generous soul and I got a sample of the killing fly (I later learned my benefactor was its creator, Frank Somers). Although there was no more action that day, the spent winged Butterfly accounted for three salmon (two to my rod) the following morning.

◆

Kim Jardine's grilse leaping in the alders high up on the Northwest Miramichi River.

Northwest Miramichi River

Of the major tributaries, I know least about the Northwest and its prime upriver tributary, the Sevogle (waters in the Northwest system are the Big and Little Sevogle, Portage, Tomogonops and the North and South Branch). I have fished both, but being a long drive from home (permanent or temporary), infrequently. What occasionally drew us to the Northwest was a large early grilse run or the compulsion to explore.

More than twenty years ago, Jim, Kim Jardine, and I endured a two-and-a-half-hour, bone-jarring, drive over logging roads to reach the headwaters of the Northwest. Here, a mighty river is but a small stream, its banks lined with alder bushes. Our 10-weight fibreglass rods were as out of place as a 60-cup aluminum coffee maker at a tea party.

This was brook trout fishing, swinging a size 10 Green Drake through small pools and in under the alders. While I connected momentarily with a grilse, which promptly jumped in the bushes and threw the fly, I later considered the ethics of harassing these salmon. Surely, I thought, after having managed to survive the gauntlet of the ocean and lower river, these fish deserved to spawn in peace, for these little streams are like the veins of a leaf which nourish a mighty trunk. Although exploring new country was worthwhile, I would not make the trip today.

The Big Sevogle is a picturesque river with many beautiful pools. I had trouble remembering any specific visits until Jim reminded me of the time we had to get him out of some serious trouble at Spruce Rock Pool. He got caught wading too deep and was unable to turn around in the current so he cast over to me near shore and I tied a big net to his line. With the net as a wading staff, he was able to move back up against the current.

Vin Swazey holds Renate Bullock's 38-pound Atlantic salmon.

Photo by Milton McKay

Author with a spring salmon on the Little Southwest Miramichi.

◆

The Bartibog

If I have only a passing acquaintance with the Northwest and its tributaries, of the Bartibog I know nothing firsthand. On the other hand, Jim claims to have seen the largest salmon of his life in the river. It was near dark and he told me he was so worried he might hook the monster that he quit fishing. The Bartibog also boasts its own noted fly tier, Benedict Theophilus "Ben" Connel, creator of the Ben's Best.

Some come to fish the Miramichi year after year and never explore the tributaries. They miss beautiful country and a variety of angling experiences. Once exposed, it is impossible to be satisfied with only one Miramichi; ever again.

Miramichi's Spring Fishery

Arguments, both face to face and in print, have erupted over the ethics and quality of angling for salmon kelts. In my view, all ethical arguments against this exploitation of the resource are specious. Without doubt, it is the most conservative of all fisheries.

Such an unequivocal statement is warranted because kelts have already served nature's primary purpose, spawning. Also, there is a low survival rate upon reaching the ocean due to predation and adjusting to the change in salinity. Further, in the cold spring water, released kelts have a very high survival rate as demonstrated by several hook-and-release research studies. Finally, few anglers keep even the legally takable grilse.

Only a fool would argue that kelts are as aesthetically pleasing as fresh-run salmon, for they have lost a third of their body weight. Regardless, as the result of feeding, their appearance improves the further downriver they are caught. As for fighting performance, a kelt's is every bit as variable as that of a fresh-run salmon. Many will jump repeatedly. On average, they take fewer and shorter runs than bright salmon, thus coming to hand a little sooner.

Spring fishing was once very popular with visiting sports and a mainstay of the commercial lodges. This began to change more than a decade ago. Although misguided adverse publicity and the grilse-only kill regulation played a role in the decline, the primary reason was a change in the character of fly fishers.

◆

Hen House Pool on the Northwest Miramichi River.

Jim Marriner plays a salmon on the Sevogle River.

◆

Once, anglers were prepared to sit in a boat and let out and then wind in a whole sinking line. While the method produces fish, it is unattractive to those accustomed to casting a fly.

Not surprisingly, such boring, sedentary tactics are unnecessary. Casting modern full sinking, sink-tip, and even floating lines under appropriate conditions, will yield plenty of hook-ups. The "secret" is to present the fly slowly and deep, accomplished by appropriate line selection, adjusting casting angles, and mending line. Bill Ensor, Mr. Tourism for New Brunswick's angling and hunting resource told me, "I've even raised a few spring salmon to big Bombers [dry flies] in the lower river." Don't count on dry flies if you want big catches however, it's strictly a "minor tactic".

While casting from shore can be quite effective, angling from a boat is best due to the increased mobility it provides. By tradition, during the spring season, the entire river is open to

all. Such freedom of movement may be critical to counter the vagaries of weather. For example, an early (or late) breakup may mean a good deal of running around to locate the bulk of the outgoing run.

The incentive to endure the changeable weather of a Miramichi "spring" is the opportunity to land a bunch of fish. For, while during the bright season anglers are permitted to catch-and-release four salmon per day, in spring there is no limit to the number one can release. With a bit of luck and a modicum of skill, anglers can expect to release 10 to 20 salmon per day providing one finds the fish. As noted earlier, kelts take the fly aggressively because they are actively feeding while dropping downriver.

Outgoing salmon search out quiet resting water during the journey. In May of 1995, after dinner at Wade's Fishing Lodge, I slipped on a pair of knee-high boots, grabbed my rod, and descended the stairs to the river's edge. The sun had set behind the far bank but the reds and oranges of a spectacular Miramichi sunset brightened my shore. I liked the look of a small point creating a stretch of quiet water for 30 yards downstream. Out went a size 2, Finnish Muddler, into the current just below the point. After only a few throws, a fine, hard fighting kelt holding in the seam took the fly positively.

While small points often produce a fish or two, the best locations for finding multiple salmon are slack water behind islands or bars, backeddies created by bends in the river, and deep slow pools. An easily overlooked holding area, shown to me by Vin Swazey, owner of Tuckaway Lodge near Boisetown, is tight to drop-offs near shore. Vin and I had success placing a bucktail within a few inches of the edge of a gravel bar in front of his camps.

Some fly fishers prefer 9- or 10-weight systems for spring angling but I am happy with an 8-weight. One concession is my choice of a tougher rod than I use for the rest of the season. The extra wall thickness offers a measure of security

◆

Atlantic salmon from the Little Southwest Miramichi.

Small point creating an eddy behind which a good spring salmon was taken. This illustrates good holding water for spring salmon. Photo by Milton McKay.

◆

when chucking sink-tip or full fast-sinking lines. Stout six-foot leaders are usually sufficient, but I have had to fine down to 10-foot, 10-pound test, under bright conditions.

Flies for spring fishing include a variety of streamers and bucktails. Bright patterns are popular. Bodies of silver and gold combine with wings of orange, white, yellow, and green. A well stocked box holds a number of local patterns supplemented with New England landlocked salmon and brook trout flies. The common denominator is hook size. Fly fishers rarely bend on anything smaller than a size 2.

To emphasize a point made earlier, spring fishing on the Miramichi may include decidedly wintry conditions. As Herb Curtis put it in *The Lone Angler*, "Labrador sent New Brunswick a gift....It was a white, feathery, cold and wet gift that Labrador had purchased at a spring clearance sale from a

◆

Main Southwest Miramichi near McNamee.

North Atlantic surplus store." To cope with such generosity, visitors should bring plenty of warm clothing and quality head-to-toe rainwear.

Once the spring season ran from mid-April to mid-May and the bright season began in mid-June. Beginning in 1996 however, the month gap has been eliminated. Although some object, when asked about conservation implications, Bill Hooper said, "No, I can't see any negative impacts on the salmon from this extension."

A final regulatory footnote; some people are surprised that spring fishing for non-residents can be more expensive than during summer and fall. The reason is the safety requirement that when angling from a boat there be a guide for each angler. Sports prepared to fish from shore may still take advantage of the one guide to three anglers ratio which prevails during the other seasons.

The Summer Season

Since the adoption of the continuous spring/summer season, summer on the Miramichi will arrive on the backs of the first run of fresh fish. Known as the Rocky Brook run, and averaging eight pounds, these salmon streak upstream through the high water headed for several brooks and headwater branches. Formerly, by regulation, the Rocky Brook salmon were seldom seen by downriver anglers. I look forward to testing the mettle of one of these first bright salmon of the season.

Why, you might ask, considering the ease with which this run ascends the river, don't larger numbers of salmon come at this time? Primarily because run timing is a big gamble. Trapped in the pools of small streams, early run salmon are exposed to many hazards while awaiting the fall spawn.

The first serious summer angling is for a large run of grilse entering the Northwest in late June. Afterwards, runs of salmon enter the main river and the tributaries throughout the summer, the timing depending on water conditions. In the early seventies, I favored early July for its strong grilse runs. Then, for nearly a decade, the better angling was later in the month. Now, early July has staged a comeback. Mid-July to mid-September are the days of the dry fly. Not exclusively of course, but salmon seem readier to take dries when daytime temperatures are higher. The tail of a pool in the evening is a sound bet.

As always, the quality of the angling depends on water conditions. An ideal summer has a few inches of rain each week to keep water levels up and constantly rising and falling. Such conditions keep the salmon alternately moving and holding, seeming to be an encouragement to take the fly.

Hot, dry summers are bad for salmon and angling. Water temperatures over 75 degrees can be lethal. At times like this the fish stack up in the mouths of cold-water brooks and around springs. Such locations are well known, many being privately owned. They are prized because, even when the river water temperatures are only warm, the cold water entering the main stream will hold fish in the area. A classic example is part of the Irving Company water on the main river near Doaktown. One July day, I stood on the club's veranda and watched scores of salmon circling about and breaking the surface in the deep pool off the mouth of Big Hole Brook. Under extreme conditions, regulations are passed to close these areas to fishing.

Some claim to be able to distinguish between salmon destined for different tributaries. Perhaps, but it takes a keener eye than mine. I see no difference between say, a salmon from the Renous and one from the Little Southwest. Regardless, it is true

Photo by John Swedberg.

Salmon swirls before being landed.

that Cains River fish are distinctive, as are members of a July run of fat, silver, main river grilse called Dollar Grilse.

Summer angling is classic Atlantic salmon fishing—floating lines cast down-and-across to cover the pools. While the number of dry fly fishers increases every year, I wager that four out of five anglers still start the day with a wet fly. Possible approaches are described in the chapter on tactics. Two slightly off-beat suggestions for when times are tough are doubling the length of your leader or working large flies with a sinking line through the heart of a deep pool. But don't blame me if neither succeeds, I offer no guarantees.

Because bright salmon do not actively feed, fly selection for the Miramichi, as elsewhere, is more art than science. Smaller sizes, worked slowly, are directionally correct as the water

Morning mist upstream from Big Hole Brook on the Main Southwest Miramichi.

Kelly's Channel on the Main Southwest Miramichi.

drops and warms, but an individual fish can turn that on its head when it goes after a spring-sized streamer ripped past its nose. It has happened to me. Inspiration? No, desperation.

Often, in July, Jim and I head for a main river pool near Upper Blackville. One side is public water, the other private. Years ago, someone nailed a big "Stop" sign to a birch tree on the private side perhaps to reinforce their ownership. We came to appreciate that sign because it marked a spot where salmon lay. The owner of that far shore was unknown to me until, in one of life's little coincidences, I met him while giving a presentation to the annual dinner of the Connecticut River Salmon Association. The pool also exhibits an interesting hydrological feature which I have encountered elsewhere. Near the head of the pool, a bogan enters on the outside of a bend. This creates a shallow diagonal step in the gravel bottom. Grilse commonly nose up to the step and are hooked as the fly swings along the edge. Easy pickings, but with a weird twist. Grilse taken from this location rarely fight well. Frequently, after being hooked, they can be merely walked up on shore.

Miramichi summers are magic. Long days offer extended hours of angling. Nights are cool regardless of daytime temperatures. Salmon are on the move. From the veranda of Miramichi Gray Rapids Lodge, as early July evenings yield to the night, I often watch the river's slick surface betray pods of salmon working upriver as schools of shad drop down. Regardless of the day's luck, this reaffirmation of the river's eternal cycle buoys the spirit for the morrow.

Fall

'The autumn always gets me badly, as it breaks into colours,' wrote D.H. Lawrence. Not so for me, fall is my favorite season on the Miramichi. Now the salmon push forward, almost disregarding water levels. Now a man may fish into dusk without the insult of hurrying the evening meal. Now the frost finishes off the pestilence of flies.

Although I don't hunt, I enjoy the company of those who seek the grouse and woodcock of Miramichi valley covers. Dogs which lie languid in the heat of summer, prance and twitch at the sight of shotguns and blaze orange and the smell of gun oil. Stories of salmon lost and landed bleed into miraculous doubles and canine feats of detection or persistence.

Crisp October mornings are the rule in the valleys. Snow is seldom seen but rime covered grasses sparkle as brightly in the early morning light. Down the western slopes spread splashes of fluorescent yellows, reds, and oranges as the sun ascends. Salmon awake and begin to leap in anticipation of the day.

Fall salmon are often more aggressive, although certainly still subject to periods of lockjaw. They also exhibit an eclectic taste in flies. Everything goes. One will take a size 14 trout fly, another a 2/0 Black Practitioner. Some fall to such ugly patterns as the Green Slime. They also succumb to a variety of presentations. At Gray Rapids Miramichi Lodge during the last two years, I or my companions have landed salmon by ripping a fly over their heads, twitching a fly as it swung across stream, upstream nymphing, speeding up or slowing down the swing of the fly by varying the angle of the cast, sinking the fly with sink-tip lines or sinking leaders, as well as the standard down-and-across approach.

Fall is also the season of the hookbill—salmon which in anticipation of spawning have already begun to experience physical changes. In the lower river, many are headed for the Cains. Changes include the growing of large kypes (a hooking

Downstream of Kelly's Channel.

Fall morning at Miramichi Gray Rapids Lodge.

◆

development of the lower and upper jaws) in the male and heavy spotting. Cains-bound salmon will already have begun to acquire the characteristic red sides.

Proximity to spawning affects a salmon's fighting spirit. While there are no absolutes, fall fish jump fewer times and the average—for a capable angler—landing time of a minute per pound is reduced by a third. The compensation is more and larger fish.

Rain is usually welcome on a salmon river, in reasonable quantities of course, and its arrival reveals a huge advantage the Miramichi has over other rivers—the size of the watershed. Should heavy rains swell the tributaries, the main river may remain fishable for several more days, by which time the

◆

Brian Roadhouse with a colorful fall grilse.

smaller streams may have begun to subside. And in some circumstances the rainfall pattern renders only certain tributaries unfishable. Only once in the last quarter century has a fall flood of biblical proportions wiped me out completely.

Does autumn enhance the mysterious connection between salmon and women? Anecdotes are hardly conclusive, but just last fall at Gray Rapids, another incident was added to the mythology. It was during the first week of October, the water was extremely low, and the salmon, while jumping and rolling constantly, were being particularly uncooperative. Across the river on the public water, eight anglers were rotating through the pool, one was female. She cast reasonably well, but certainly no better than the others, and the fly she was using was soon being tied to several leaders. Regardless, in the space of three hours, she landed two salmon while the entire male contingent managed but one.

During the last several years, the open season has been gradually extended to the fifteenth of October. And it has become the most popular time for many anglers. So much so that it can be difficult to get reservations at the lodges with the best water. No wonder, for when the rains finally arrived in the fall of 1995 (after the season had closed), observers reported thousands of salmon barrelling up the river, including many estimated to weigh over 30 pounds.

Guides

"Years ago I had a sport fishing Mountain Channel when old Tom Boyd owned Mountain Channel Lodge. The sport had been casting for a couple of hours and asked me to take a few casts. I said no because I felt the sun was coming right to fish a lie where I knew a salmon was holding and I wanted the sport to catch it. But he insisted and so finally I took the rod. The first thing I did was cut off his fly and tie on an identical one from my box.

"Sure enough, a few casts later, I hooked the salmon and handed the sport the rod. After I netted and killed the fish, the sport looked me in the eye and said, 'That's the same pattern I had on, why did you change flies?' 'You're wrong,' I said, 'it's not the same, your fly is for the other side of the river.'

"The sport headed up the steps to the lodge for lunch and I stayed behind to clean the salmon. Then I headed up the steps with the fish. When I got to the top of the bank, old Boyd was waiting for me, and he was hopping mad. 'You're fired,' he told me, 'Your sport just gave me hell for selling him flies for the wrong side of the river.' In the end I kept my job but old Boyd never did see the humour of the situation."

This wonderful example of Miramichi wit comes courtesy of Percy Mountain, now head guide at Gray Rapids Miramichi Lodge. Percy has guided for nearly 50 years in addition to a lengthy stint as a federal warden. The latter providing him with plenty of hair-raising tales of tense encounters with poachers.

As in any profession, there are excellent, mediocre, and poor Atlantic salmon guides. Sadly, many visiting anglers don't understand what makes a good one. A great salmon guide doesn't stand at your elbow giving instructions. His task, beyond knowing the taking lies in his pools, how to cast to them, the best flies for different conditions, and how to get a salmon to hand, is to watch the water for signs of salmon and be alert to slight changes in conditions. Sometimes their sixth sense borders on the supernatural.

Consider this recent first-hand experience. Although there were hundreds of salmon about, the river was extremely low and the fish very reluctant. Just upstream of me, Percy's sport was casting to several salmon lying in shallow water near shore. After about an hour, Percy got up from his chair on the bank and walked over to the angler. He changed the fly and

Releasing a salmon at the Miramichi Gray Rapids Lodge.

directed the next cast. As if marching to orders, a 12-pound Atlantic swallowed that fly on the first swing. Was it a magic fly? No, none of the dozens of other fish which later watched it pass overhead was interested. Simply the right fly, at the right moment, swinging the right way over the right salmon!

I was not fortunate enough to have family or friends who could serve as a guide, fulfilling the legal obligation for a non-resident, my contacts with other professional Miramichi guides have been limited, somy contact with other professional Miramichi guides has been limited. But I know that many hundreds of superb guides have spent a lifetime of seasons putting sports in contact with Atlantic salmon. Certain families along the river have been guiding for five generations. Mentioning some would only mean omitting others.

There is an old proverb, 'Want of wit is worse than want of gear.' As proof, while many Miramichi natives may have wanted for possessions, their wit is bountiful. Some guiding anecdotes already in print are too delicious to leave hidden among the shelves of book collectors. Take the following com-

Percy Mountain, head guide at Miramichi Gray Rapids Lodge, nets a salmon.

A little Miramichi wit.

ment of Bert Pond, related in Jack Russell's *Jill and I and the Salmon*. When hooked by the fly of a sport, and after ripping the offending hook from his neck, the laconic Bert said, "That's the first time I've riz to that fly this year."

One of my favorite quips is found in *Life on the Miramichi* by Clayton Stanley Stewart. Stewart was one of the early (late '30s) fishing outfitters on the river with his first camp at Hayesville, a few miles upriver from Boisetown. A little more than a decade later he was running the largest operation on the Miramichi. Oh, yes, the story.

Seems two sports and their guides were proceeding along a woods path. One of the anglers was quite portly and lagged behind. Stepping off the path to answer a call of nature landed him in a bog hole, into which he promptly sank to his waist. Answering his cries for help, the other three returned. The two anglers were understandably agitated. After rolling a cigarette, taking a few puffs, and surveying the situation, the mired angler's guide suggested, "Well, he is pretty heavy and might be hard to pull out. It would be easier to just push him down a little farther, and leave him there." After a moments stunned silence, the guide allowed as, "Well maybe we should pull him out, it would look bad to leave him there."

Speaking of guides always brings the canoe and setting pole to mind. One evening, after a tour of the attractive new facilities of Black Rapids Salmon Club, Bill Ensor and I walked to the river bank. The owner, George Curtis, saw us from the far side of the river and poled across the rapids to meet us. In the low water, his effortless progress among the rocks belied a lifetime of experience. George is the son of Roy Curtis, perhaps the most widely known guide on the river during his lifetime. For over 30 years, Roy looked after Ted Williams' camp and was Ted's personal guide.

To run the river with an expert in the use of the pole is an inspiring experience. Ferrying through Big Louie rapids, the canoe moving side to side as easily as if one were walking down a rocky slope, is a testament to a skill not easily acquired. And knowing the result of hanging on a stuck pole for a fraction too long adds an extra thrill. More than once, the sight of an upright pole, vibrating with the current in the middle of a rapids, has set me speculating on the fate of its owner.

Fly Tiers of the Miramichi

Dealing with people—be they anglers, fly tiers, or guides—in the story of a river with almost two centuries of angling history is an author's minefield. Some important contributors will be overlooked. It is as inevitable as tomorrow. When considering tiers, my most serious omission is the scores who have toiled producing commercial flies but whose names have never been associated with a pattern. Many of these men and women are (or were) superb craftspersons. The story of one of the best, Wallace Doak, and his son Jerry, is told in the chapter on fly shops.

Traversing the rapids.

Wallace W. Doak outside his original store located in Doaktown. Photo by Jerry Doak.

◆

Two men who have spent considerable time and effort researching the fly tiers of New Brunswick are Dewey Gillespie and W.F. "Budd" Kitchen from Miramichi City. The result is an exhibition entitled, "Where the Rivers Meet." A book summarizing the collected material is anticipated. I profited from their labor in preparing this chapter.

The barbershop was, and still is outside of suburbia, a bastion of maleness. In fishing country, it often rivals the fly shop for information. Sometimes, as happened to me on the Little Southwest when searching to augment my supply of a killing fly, the wares of local tiers can be found tucked away in a corner. Although difficult to prove, evidence suggests that one D'Arcy L. "Doris" O'Donnell (1886-1948), a barber, was the first commercial fly tier on the Miramichi. O'Donnell operated a barber shop, restaurant, and tackle shop in Doaktown and was selling his own flies as early as 1924.

Many well-known angler/fly tiers from the northeastern United States travel(led) to the Miramichi for their Atlantic salmon angling. Some developed patterns for the river but few of these have achieved significant popularity. Names such as John (Jack) Atherton, Charles DeFeo, Keith Fulsher, and Charles Krom will be familiar.

The story of Ira Gruber is told in *Atlantic Salmon Flies & Fishing* by Joe Bates (recently updated with improved color plates and reissued by Stackpole Books). Gruber retired from Pennsylvania to the Miramichi in 1915 and spent better than 30 years working on angling methods and fly patterns. Bates credits him with developing the distinctive conformation of Miramichi flies, i.e. slim, short, cigar shaped body, sparse hackle, short, low-angled wing, and fine tinsel ribbing. Four of his patterns are the Black Spider, Blackhawk, Oriole, and Reliable.

Although Bates attributed the Miramichi style to Ira Gruber, a reasonable case can be made to share this honor with the man who taught him to tie flies, Everett Price (1893-1962). A native Miramicher, Price began tying in the early 30s and taught many local people to tie. Some of his patterns are The Rose of New England, Price's Dose, Black Squirrel, and Buttermilk Brown.

Bert Miner (1907-1969) of Doaktown was a contemporary of Everett Price and it is likely that cross-fertilization occurred between all the tiers of that era. Miner was a Cains specialist and his most famous fly, the Copper Killer, reflects the fact that that river's salmon seem to prefer a somewhat stained fly. Other Miner patterns which live on are the Cains River, Blackville, and Silver Down-Easter.

◆

Marc Madore, fly tier and guide.

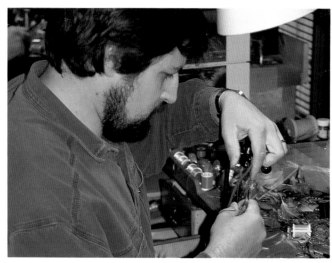

Jerry Doak at the bench.

◆

Far up the Miramichi, near Juniper, Fred Grant and his family produced salmon flies for many years. Without knowing it, numbers of northeastern U.S. salmon anglers owed their success to Grant's flies, for one of his largest customers was Abercrombie & Fitch. Grant developed few of his own patterns and the only one I could discover was the Grant Special, an original example of which is included in the color plate.

In 1956, while in Blackville, Maurice Ingalls, from Fort Lauderdale, Florida, developed the pattern which has killed more grilse for me over the years than all other flies combined. Conversely, my Butterflies have not been nearly as successful at attracting MSW salmon. With its divided, rearward slanted, white wings, it is best fished with imparted motion to cause the wings to pulsate.

In 1993, while fishing the Upper Oxbow pool of the Little Southwest from Debbie Norton's lodge, I was introduced to a Butterfly variation developed by Frank Somers featuring sparse, yellow wings tied spent, and a short Krystal Flash tail. It proved itself there—and in several other locations since—for MSW salmon. Frank lives on the banks of the Northwest and supplies flies to several outfitters and private clubs as well as a number of small shops in the area.

Jack Sullivan tied many thousands of Butterflies, as well as other popular flies, in his camp at Upper Blackville, between Blackville and Doaktown. As noted elsewhere, he was a supplier to W.W. Doak. Sullivan was an outfitter in the summer and, according to Wayne Curtis, a superb caster and slow water specialist.

Only a year before his death, I interviewed Father Elmer J. Smith, then living near Fredericton, about his famous creation, The Bomber. By the time I spoke to him he had modified the fly and, surprisingly, dropped the trademark single, forward slanting wing. The accompanying photograph shows the most recent version. Father Smith also originated The Priest, an all-white wet fly which is still popular when a startling departure from the standard flies seems appropriate.

"We considered several areas, but finally chose Blackville as the best overall location for a sportsman," said Marc Madore as we gathered in his fly-tying room. After a full career on the move with the military, Marc has already established himself as one of the region's premier tiers of both classic and modern salmon flies. In the fall of 1995, struggling under tough low-water conditions, his Shrimp was the only fly to produce for me. Marc originated and tied this *River Journal*'s signature fly, The Miramichi R.J.

Another recent homesteader and guide is former railroader, Larry Tracey. Although Larry isn't a commercial tier, he developed one of the most successful fall flies in recent years, the LT Special. "My goal was to make a fly that included all the fall colors," said Larry, "and it worked right away for me and my clients." The LT Special has regularly delivered hook-ups for us during the fall season.

◆

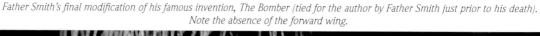

Father Smith's final modification of his famous invention, The Bomber (tied for the author by Father Smith just prior to his death).
Note the absence of the forward wing.

Four editions of The Bomber.

Barrie Duffield, who along with his wife Joan operates Burntland Brook Lodge in Boisetown, moved to the Miramichi from the Nashwaak River three years ago. "I've been tying flies for nearly 35 years," Barry told me before we began talking about his most successful creation, the Burdock. "It's patterned after the Wulff series but tied almost entirely with deer hair. I've taken numbers of salmon with it in sizes 6 to 10 depending on water height and temperature." And the Burdock has an impressive reputation on big trout as well, having seduced several over five pounds in the last two years. Barry also dresses a small, black dry fly with a touch of green to imitate a hatch which occurs during cool, damp, calm weather from late August to October. On several occasions he has witnessed a pool full of salmon rising to this fly and his imitation has scored well.

"I became interested in fly tying when I couldn't find the variants which I was convinced would work for non-taking fish," said Renate Bullock of Boisetown. Renate guides for Tuckaway Lodge and had her first fly-tying lessons in the early 80s from guests of the lodge from New Jersey. "My techniques were honed during sessions with Warren Duncan, who is a family friend," she continued. Warren, who lives in Saint John, New Brunswick, is an internationally recognized salmon fly tier. "Perhaps my biggest personal discovery was the increased effectiveness of flies with a single strand of flash material added to the wing, although it doesn't always work of course," said Renate when quizzed about her developments. Renate's capture of a 38-pound salmon on her own pattern is documented elsewhere.

Wrapping up, I once again apologize to those tiers not included in this chapter. Some may say with justification, "my contributions are more important than some mentioned." Or even, Heaven forbid, that that lad Marriner has this bit all wrong.

Flies for the Miramichi

No one knows why an Atlantic salmon will take one fly and not another. This wonderful (or cursed, depending on whether you are buying or selling) uncertainty has led to a profusion of patterns throughout history. The creative urge has yet to be stilled. There are no rules, almost. For the Miramichi, flies must by regulation be tied on double or single hooks without added weight.

Some patterns go swiftly from stardom to obscurity, some go on and on. Without question, the Miramichi's most enduring pattern is the Black Bear and its variations. Tied on single and double hooks, normally in sizes 4 to 12, with red, green, or orange butts (or combinations of the foregoing), it is the staple of the angler's box. To my knowledge it has never been convincingly attributed. On the river the fly is referred to simply by the color of the butt; thus to the question, "What are you using?", "A size 6 double Green Butt," is a complete answer.

Perhaps the greatest gift the Miramichi has given to salmon anglers is The Bomber, now used all over the world for dozens of species. Bugs, sometimes called Buck Bugs, are wet fly derivatives of The Bomber and are hugely popular. The Miramichi is a "green" river, thus, the Green Machine, a green Bug, is very productive. Another fly which has its innings is the Shady Lady, a black Bug. The first Bugs I used were plump of body like The Bomber (and often fished dry or damp), but to keep up with the times they joined Weight Watchers and today's versions are much slimmer. Bugs exhibit one other departure from standard practice, they are generally tied on extra-stout, down-eyed, bronzed, trout wet fly hooks as opposed to the classic black, up-eyed salmon irons.

Many flies were discussed in the chapter about tiers, so I will simply state what I consider to be the essential box of the

Milton McKay spring fishing during a snowstorm on the Main Southwest Miramichi.

Miramichi salmon angler. It is remotely possible that some may not agree!

Wet Flies

Black Bear, red and green butt, sizes 2 to 14, single and double.

Butterfly, red and green butt, sizes 6 to 12, single and double.

Butterfly, yellow horizontal wings, sizes 6 to 10, single.

Cosseboom, sizes 2 to 8, single.

Green Machine, (with and without gold Krystal Flash tail), sizes 4 to 10, single.

Shady Lady (with and without gold Krystal Flash tail), sizes 4 to 8, single.

General Practitioner, Standard and Black, sizes 1/0 to 4, single.

LT Special, sizes 2 to 8, single (for fall fishing).

Any thinly dressed black fly, sizes 12 and 14.

A personal favorite is the Green Drake, because it killed my first MSW salmon. The fly has continued to be a steady, if not prolific taker, and for example, recently killed my first Scottish salmon. The pattern is not included in the above list as it is not particularly popular today. However, strangely enough, Phair, in his 1938 classic, *Atlantic Salmon Fishing*, credits it as the essential fly for the Miramichi.

Although black and green are the river's primary colors, there are times when a white or yellow fly is the only answer. At such times I choose The Priest (white) or the GW Special (greenish yellow) by Gerry Williamson. Also, in addition to those specifically mentioned, believers modify other patterns in the list by adding a little flash to the wing or tail.

Finally, many patterns may be tied in low water versions. This simply means that while the hook is kept at normal size, the fly is tied on the front half of the hook only. Frankly, I pre-

fer to simply use a smaller fly, but some folks are uncomfortable with hooks smaller than a size 8.

Dry Flies

The Bomber, white with orange hackle, natural with brown hackle, brown with orange hackle, sizes 2 to 8.

Wulffs, white and grey, sizes 4 to 12.

MacIntosh, sizes 4 to 10.

Rat Faced MacDougall, sizes 6 to 12.

Any small black dry fly, sizes 12 and 14.

Spring Flies

Most spring flies have three things in common, they are streamers or bucktails, they are large, and are colorful. In addition to the following short list, I have had success with bright steelhead flies and several local patterns.

Mickey Finn, sizes 2/0 to 2.

Grey Ghost, sizes 2/0 to 2.

Marabou Muddlers, colors to please, sizes 2/0 to 6.

Other popular flies should be mentioned if only for their wonderful names. One can only suppose the history of flies such as The Rose of New England (Everett Price), Chief Needahbeh (named after the creator), and Golden Eagle, is as colorful as the patterns.

Commercial Lodges

Twenty-one Miramichi commercial lodges are listed in the current edition of the New Brunswick government *Aim and*

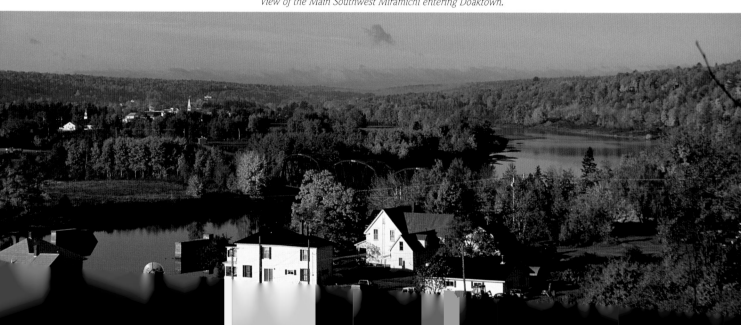

View of the Main Southwest Miramichi entering Doaktown.

Sixty-eight years of memories grace Wilson's Sporting Camps.

◆

Angle Adventures publication. I have visited several, but by no means all. Some have been very helpful in the preparation of this book, others might have been if asked. Some are relatively new, others have been established for many years.

As it is clearly impossible to write about them all, I made the arbitrary decision to provide thumbnail sketches of those that have been in operation for more than 25 years. Such lodges clearly have strong historical ties to the valley. Regardless, my decision should not be considered a comment on the quality of those excluded.

Old River Lodge

The rows of canoes rocked quietly beside the dock as we walked down the hill from the main building of Old River Lodge on our way to explore several miles of the main Miramichi east of Doaktown. Erected in 1958 by a local resident, Arlington Bamford, and expanded during the next decade, Old River was purchased by Alex Mills and Vicki Oland-Mills in 1976. "We've concentrated on upgrading the facilities and acquiring additional pools," said Alex when asked about the changes he and Vicki have made.

The Atlantic salmon is a political species, and always has been. Considering the Mills' long-time involvement in conservation organizations, my visits to Old River regularly yield insights into the latest tactics in the constant battle to save the salmon. I also recall a visit several years ago when, with a prominent editor in tow and desperately looking for a salmon during the depths of a drought, only Alex was able to find us a fish.

Upper Oxbow Angling Adventures

"My dad, Harry Blackmore, started taking guests in 1928," Debbie Norton told me. Harry built several cabins on the banks of the Little Southwest some 10 miles upriver from Red Bank to house his sports. While the interiors have been modernized, the original structures have stood the test of time. Late one evening, lulled into a semi-torpor by a satisfying meal and a roaring fire, I felt connected to those first, likely long-dead, anglers who had gazed upon these same stones and logs after a successful day on the river.

"In those days the attraction was the spring fishing," Debbie explained as we chatted, "and the guides would pole the sports 10 miles up or down the river looking for the best fishing." Today, Debbie and husband Dale welcome guests throughout the season. Although he guides irregularly, we were fortunate to have Fred Blackmore, Debbie's older brother, by our side. As is my usual practice, I pumped Fred for his fishing experiences. "I used to love salmon fishing but gave it up when the runs dried up," Fred admitted, "but seeing you fellows catch fish again is getting me a bit stirred up." And when we were done for the morning he accepted the offer to try a few casts with my rod.

Wade's Fishing Lodge

"Perhaps the most unique thing about Wade's is the length of time the employees have stayed with the lodge," says George Holmes, a member of the syndicate which purchased the operation about five years ago. "For example, one of our guides,

Jimmy Colford, has been here for 40 years and his sister, Dorothy McCormack, has cooked for the lodge for 30 years." In 1994, Dorothy received recognition for her accomplishments when she was inducted into the Miramichi Salmon Museum's Hall of Fame.

In 1933, just downriver from the mouth of the Cains, Charlie Wade opened his lodge for business. Eventually, Charlie's son Herb took control of the operation. The family ownership was continuous except for a two year period in the 70s when it was owned by Standard Oil. Recently, the present owners purchased and restored a nearby private camp on the Cains built in 1933 by an American, Admiral Merril.

During my stay at Wade's, an unusual discovery helped me repay George's hospitality. One evening while browsing the reading material in our cabin, I stumbled upon a gem amongst the usual dross, a signed copy of Lee Wulff's *Leaping Silver*. The next morning I suggested to George that he might consider keeping the valuable volume in a somewhat less exposed location!

Pond's Resort

Ellis Pond began taking in sports to fish the Miramichi in 1925. Today, his great-grandson, Keith, with wife Linda, run the largest complex on the river at Ludlow, near Boisetown. In between, Keith's grandfather Elmer and father, Charlie, maintained the Pond tradition. At the close of the World War I, even before his dad started the business, Elmer was guiding canoe trips on the upper river in the summer months. In those days there were no permanent camps and guides and sports stayed in tents as they ran the river. Because the canoes could not carry enough supplies for the whole trip, local men would pole loaded canoes from Ludlow to Push-and-be-Damned rapids in May, an exciting trip in the flood waters of spring.

"Until the 1950s, most of the salmon fishing was from canoes," Keith told me. "The most popular makes were Ogilvies and Millers, although my great-granddad Ellis made a number of his own canvas canoes." In 1981, Keith purchased the famous Russell camps built by Elmer Pond and located just across the road from the main resort. To offer a wilderness experience to their guests, they also acquired the lease on 13 miles of the upper river and purchased camps at McKiel Brook and Moose Call.

Wilson's Sporting Camps

"We've traced our family's connection to outfitting on the Miramichi to my great-grandfather's great-aunt Agnes Wilson," said Keith Wilson. "She seems to have been hosting anglers in the spring and fall from England and New York City back in the 1880s." But the unbroken tradition of Wilson's stretches from 1928 when Keith's great-grandfather, Willard W. Wilson, opened for business in the same location occupied today.

The Wilson water at McNamee includes some of the most beautiful, classic, braided water salmon pools on the river. And they maintain several of the traditional ways abandoned by other lodges such as the shore lunch carried in pails first used by Keith's grandfather. Another unique Wilson's touch is naming their cabins after long-time guests such as Stanley Church. "I believe Mr. Church has been coming here the longest, twice a year for 49 years," said Keith. I should be so lucky!

Governor's Table Lodge

A few hundred yards up the South Branch from the Forks Pool where the Main Southwest Miramichi is born, "Hoot" and Charlene Smith have operated Governor's Table since 1960. "The main building was originally a private camp and we added the cabins gradually over the years," replied Hoot when asked about the lodge's history. While Governor's Table is the oldest angling camp still operating around Juniper, Hoot told me that the Sweet brothers, the McKenzie's, and Gordon Tweedie operated camps in this area in the '20s. Before the Irving Company acquired the land and restricted access, sports were taken up the North Branch to Beadle Brook, famous for trout.

I was in for a real surprise when Hoot answered a question about the earliest fresh-run salmon he had seen. "About June 6th," he said. That's only a week or so after the main run of sea trout shows up in the area. "But usually our first salmon arrive around the end of June."

Tuckaway Cabins

"After years of cooking for a number of lodges on the river, my dad Fred opened Tuckaway in 1939," said Vin Swazey. It seems salmon fishing was a pretty good deal in those days. Vin recalled that $5.00 would get you full accommodation and a day's angling from a canoe with a personal guide. In those days, because the number of anglers was limited and almost all fishing was from canoes, guides had free access to most of the river.

In addition to running his own business, Vin operated Camp Thomas for 15 years for the corporate owners. Located at Mountain Channel, downstream from Blackville, Camp Thomas was once a noted commercial lodge operated by the Boyd family. Many old-timers on the river consider the home pool at Mountain Channel to be one of the best on the Miramichi.

After a successful day of spring salmon fishing, Vin told us the story of a photograph hanging on the wall of our Tuckaway cabin. Therein, Vin is holding a huge salmon and sporting an equally huge smile. "I netted that salmon for one of my guides, Renate Bullock," Vin recounted, "and it weighed in at 38 pounds. She hooked it on one of her own patterns, the RB, on September 7, 1986." Just another example of the propensity of very large salmon to favor female anglers.

Fly Shops

W.W. Doak

Located in Doaktown, "A Miramichi Tradition" is the motto for the Miramichi's best known fly shop. In the late

The new W.W. Doak Fly Shop.

◆

thirties W(allace) W(ard) Doak started selling personally-tied salmon flies from the attic of a shed at his mother's home. A few years later he built a little shop at the front of his new home on Main Street. Little did he suspect it was destined to become a landmark for salmon anglers from all over the world.

Jerry Doak started working for his dad when he was 10 but, with an employer whose views on quality were uncompromising, did not begin to tie flies for sale until he was 16. In 1977, faced with the terminal illness of his dad, Jerry returned home from university to run the family business. His decision meant the traditions of W.W. Doak would continue.

In Doak's catalog you will find the business's approach to flies. 'Our reputation for high quality locally tied salmon flies is the basis upon which our family business has been developed over the past fifty years. We continue to be mindful of the standard of excellence established by my father during his life time and we diligently seek to preserve this standard by carefully inspecting every fly we sell. We are privileged to have had a group of skilled New Brunswick craftsmen with us over the years, and their pride and talent is reflected in the quality of their workmanship.' I asked Jerry if there were any familiar names among those who have supplied flies for the store. "Sure," he said, "Maurice Ingalls, inventor of the Butterfly, and closely associated with the commercial success of the Bomber, tied for Dad in the mid 60s and, while perhaps not internationally recognized, Jack Sullivan was also a supplier."

In 1987, while it appeared certain that operating out of the original little store would remain safe and profitable, Jerry felt that customer service demanded larger quarters. Luckily, an old home down the street became available. After four months of major renovations, a Miramichi tradition relocated.

I once asked Jerry if his success had motivated him to try some of the world's other salmon rivers. His reply was uncompromising, "With the greatest Atlantic salmon river in the world at my back door, I've never felt much urge to travel."

On my last trip to the Miramichi, after asking Jerry to provide the majority of the fly patterns for this *River Journal*, and not wishing to shatter my own 25 year tradition, I bought a few little items before leaving the premises of W.W. Doak.

George's Fly Shop

Almost beneath the railway bridge that crosses the Renous near Quarryville Pool is George Rutledge's shop. The shop takes me back to the "good old days" before fly fishing became "big

◆

George's Fly Shop located in Quarryville.

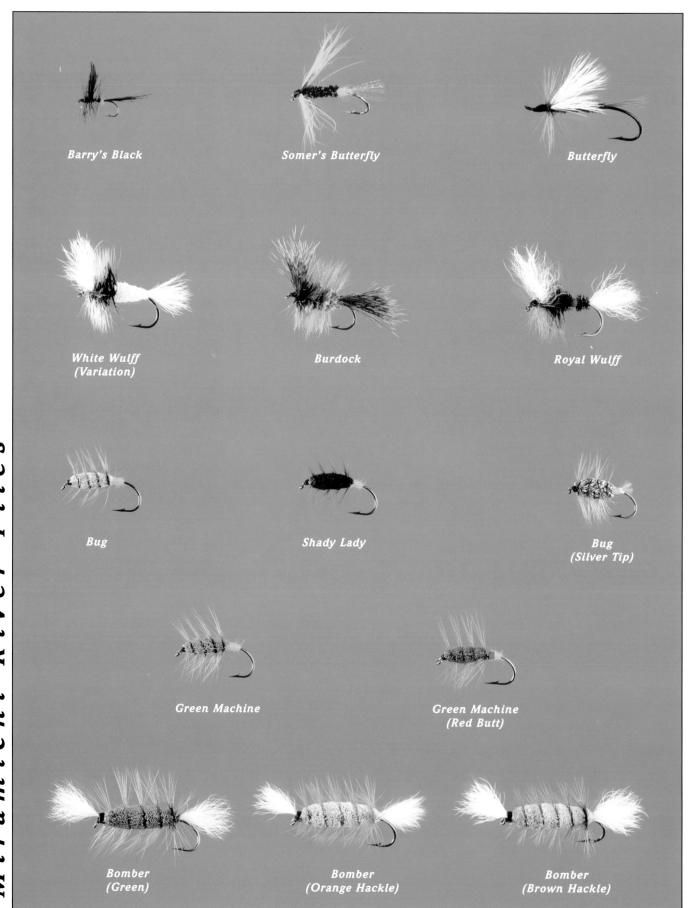

Barry's Black

Somer's Butterfly

Butterfly

White Wulff
(Variation)

Burdock

Royal Wulff

Bug

Shady Lady

Bug
(Silver Tip)

Green Machine

Green Machine
(Red Butt)

Bomber
(Green)

Bomber
(Orange Hackle)

Bomber
(Brown Hackle)

Miramichi River Flies

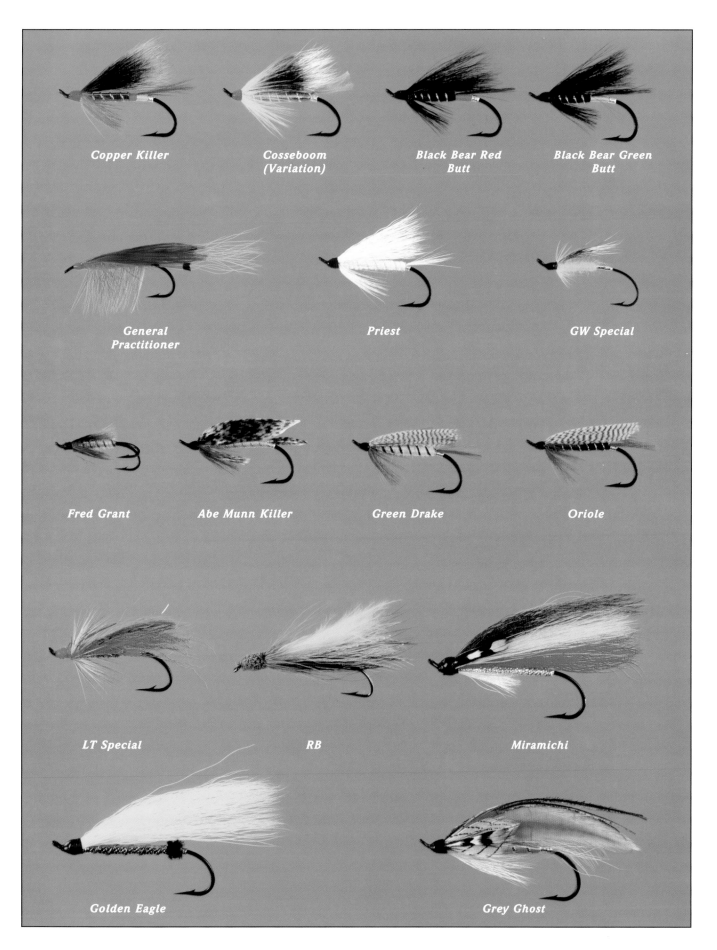

Copper Killer

Cosseboom (Variation)

Black Bear Red Butt

Black Bear Green Butt

General Practitioner

Priest

GW Special

Fred Grant

Abe Munn Killer

Green Drake

Oriole

LT Special

RB

Miramichi

Golden Eagle

Grey Ghost

Red fox. Photo by Milton McKay.

business". Crowded with flies, materials, and tackle, it reminds me of my den. Amazingly, George can lay his hands on a myriad of obscure products, but I'm sure a visiting inventory control expert would have a seizure.

The atmosphere is old-time as well—George behind the counter and a couple of anglers lounging on the other side talking salmon. If you want to know what's going to happen up-river, visit George's, for it's at the Quarryville pool that a run of fresh fish fall for the first fly. One autumn, when the word wafted up-river that the Slime Fly was scoring heavily, it was to George's that I headed for a sample and the required material.

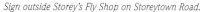

Sign outside Storey's Fly Shop on Storeytown Road.

Storey's Fly Shop

Up Storeytown Road, on the north side of the Miramichi (across from Doaktown), the observant angler will spot a white sign announcing the location of Storey's Fly Shop. "I used to tie flies for Murray Ward who owned a shop in Chipman," said Cedric Storey who guides for Wilson's Sporting Camps. "When Murray closed up in '87 he offered me his stock so I converted our woodshed into a small shop. My wife Jean runs it." The small red building is as neat as the white house in front. Although obviously not constantly manned, a knock on the back door of the house will get a pleasant response.

Pond's Resort

Pond's has an Orvis outlet as part of their service to guests and visitors. The selection is not extensive but they carry the necessities. Although I have not personally inspected the stock, Bill Ensor tells me that the quality of Pond's flies is excellent.

General

Common to most areas with major fly fisheries, many stores and gas stations have cards of salmon flies for sale. A few of the most popular patterns and sizes are usually available but the selection is limited. Also, since the tiers are anonymous, the quality is always, although not necessarily fairly, suspect.

Other Flora and Fauna

A few years ago, we sat on the front veranda of Old River Lodge in the noontime heat of a sunny, summer's day lamenting the state of salmon angling. Suddenly, one of nature's finest fishers put the lie to our complaints. Swooping from high above, an osprey neatly plucked a grilse from the surface of the home pool. At the time, a unique experience, as for many years the great bird had been absent from the valley. It is generally agreed, even though the recovery period has been lengthy, that the ending of DDT spraying was the catalyst for the return of the species.

Over the years I have seen most of the valley's non-human inhabitants, some much more often than others. Deer, black bear, moose, foxes, beaver, muskrat, mink, otter, coyotes roam the woods and waterways and skunks and porcupines play merry hell with inexperienced dogs. Perhaps even an ephemeral eastern panther may be found in the headwaters country. Covers shelter migrating woodcock, and ruffed and spruce grouse. Mergansers, black ducks, and Canada geese are seen in season. Songbirds, raptors, and woodpeckers are common summer sights. The lower Miramichi valley is settled, but the wildlife hung in and adjusted.

Flora

Although I have no clear recollection, I suspect my high school biology course was truncated. While the names of trees come readily to mind, woodland plants and wildflowers are a mystery. I do recognize immature ferns, called fiddleheads, but only because they end up on my plate as a celebrated vegetable.

As for the big stuff, the Miramichi's valleys bristle with spruce, pine, maple, birch, poplar, ash, beech, and others. Of course, most of the great softwoods that once dominated the region have long since fallen to axe or chainsaw. Even so, high on a wilderness ridge, one may still find a giant white pine, the

Boxberry (aka Bunchberry).

longtime prize of the valley, that has somehow escaped death by fire or saw.

Conservation

As the Atlantic salmon resource of Eastern Canada slid toward extinction after 1968 due to the Newfoundland and Greenland commercial fisheries, the initial response was to gradually reduce catch limits. When this didn't work, a key decision for the Miramichi was made in 1984. In this year much of the commercial fishery was closed and anglers were required to release all salmon above 25 inches. Today, most commercial licenses have been bought out.

The Atlantic Salmon Federation (ASF) applied constant pressure to ensure such actions were undertaken. The ASF is

Within the banks of the Miramichi hide many pleasingly strange natural wonders.

Students measuring salmon at the Palisades Catch and Release Area, North Pole Brook.

Barrier fence on the North Branch, Main Southwest Miramichi.

◆

the primary and largest organization dedicated to the preservation and enhancement of Atlantic salmon in North America. From its headquarters and laboratory in St. Andrews, New Brunswick, it undertakes and funds studies and enhancement projects and lobbies governments and international regulatory bodies to implement conservation strategies.

The measures started a recovery and have been extended continuously since their introduction. In 1992 the commercial closure and buy-out program was widened to include the interception net fisheries in Newfoundland and Labrador. Finally, due to the tireless efforts and financial commitment of Iceland's Orri Vigfusson, the Greenland salmon quota was purchased for several years. Confounding factors have prevented the expected extent of the recovery (still far from the 1/2 million of 1966-67) but the average size of the fish hooked in the Miramichi has increased substantially. Bill Hooper attributes the latter phenomenon to the increased number of repeat spawners in the returning population.

"Our juvenile stocks in the Miramichi are the healthiest they've been in several decades," says Hooper. "Unfortunately we now seem to have a serious problem with post-smolt survival at sea." Normally one expects an 8 to 15 percent survival rate but lately this critical factor is closer to 2 to 3 percent. A number of explanations for this problem have been advanced but none is universally accepted. A recent conference on the subject indicated colder water temperatures in the southern Labrador Sea might be responsible.

The above measures might be termed "macro management", as they affect many rivers. On a micro, or river specific, level there have also been a number of initiatives. One is the advent of in-stream satellite rearing stations established by the federal Department of Fisheries and Oceans in co-operation

with a number of riparian owners with suitable habitat on their property. The initial facility was built in 1984 on Rocky Brook Club property followed in 1985 by a second at one of the Black Brook Club sites. A major program expansion took place in 1991 and there are now 16 sites. While this program enjoys widespread support, it is not without controversy. Legitimate concerns include the possibility of disease, genetic dilution and adverse impacts on wild fish present.

Another, more expensive, undertaking is the barrier fences on the North Branch of the Main Southwest, and in the headwaters of the Dungarvon and Northwest. Here, guarded 24 hours a day, salmon are held in deep cold-water pools until just before they are ready to spawn. The primary purpose is to thwart poachers. The fences also serve as counting stations to monitor the health of the returning run.

The Miramichi Salmon Association (MSA) has been a major force for protection and enhancement of the Miramichi salmon resource since its formation in 1953. Headquartered in Boisetown, its over 1100 members are drawn from all interested segments of the Miramichi family; residents, guides, individual anglers, outfitters, private camp owners, clubs, and corporations. The MSA played a leading role in the successful effort to ban DDT spraying, led efforts to tag salmon, and lobbied aggressively in support of the critical commercial fishing and angling regulation changes discussed previously. The association has also helped support studies into the affects of open season changes and forestry practices, and funds marine biology scholarships. A major undertaking has been the MSA's financial support for the aforementioned satellite fry rearing stations.

The New Brunswick Wildlife Federation has also been very active in conservation activities on the Miramichi. Both my brother Jim, who was Federation president and then Executive

Conservation sign.

◆

Director for a number of years, and Gerry Williamson spent many hours manning the counting fence on the Bartholomew. The Federation also participates with other organizations in a variety of salmon and habitat enhancement projects.

As elsewhere, some aboriginal fisheries continue to cause concern. Native leaders have negotiated a number of agreements and some, such as with the Redbank band, have been very successful. But a recent clash involving some disenchanted youth of another band, backed by armed outside agitators, revealed the fragility of these arrangements.

Forestry practices have an immense influence on spawning areas. While by no means perfect, the major New Brunswick companies are at least sensitive to the damage their activities cause the land. They have responded by reducing the size of clearcuts, accessing these in the least harmful manner, leaving larger buffer strips and being more selective in the areas to be cut. More needs to be done, particularly on unregulated private woodlots, but the situation has improved considerably over that existing a decade ago.

One nagging concern is the question of aerial spraying to combat the spruce budworm. Managed spruce forests are very susceptible to attack by this insect and the resulting destruction is unacceptable if a sustainable industry is to be maintained. Unfortunately, until a biological control strategy can completely replace chemical means, some spraying must continue.

Mining operations pose a serious threat to the immediate health of some rivers. This has been demonstrated twice in recent memory. The latest incident, a spill on the Tomogonops in 1991, decimated the populations of all living creatures in this Northwest tributary and severely affected the Northwest itself. The recovery from this disaster, although advanced, is not yet complete.

On the human side of the equation, poaching remains a threat to full recovery. With widespread reductions in the allocation of scarce government money to the protection of natural resources, this scourge may once again be on the increase. Education of the younger generation, vigilant anglers, and a less tolerant attitude by the courts to violators, remain the most cost effective means of combatting this threat.

The battle to protect and enhance the Miramichi's Atlantic salmon resource is never-ending. True, much has been accomplished and few would contest that the fishery is in far better shape than it was in the early 1980s. Regardless, any slackening of the effort could see all this good work rapidly undone. Continued cooperation of all interested parties is essential to success.

The Miramichi Salmon Museum

Great clouds of smoke and sheets of flame engulfed the forest and the river hissed and steamed like a hot spring from the fall of burning embers. Such was the view from the present day site of the Miramichi Salmon Museum of the massive conflagration which razed the Miramichi valley in October of 1825. Newspaper accounts of this human and ecological tragedy are

◆

Conservation sign at the Palisades Catch and Release Area, North Pole Brook.

Wallace Doak's original fly tying bench now housed in the Atlantic Salmon Museum.

◆

among the exhibits greeting the visitor to this outstanding conservator of the river's salmon fishing history. Although recently renamed, The Atlantic Salmon Museum on the Miramichi, I retained the original, more familiar, name for this *River Journal*.

Historically the centre of the Miramichi sport fishery, Doaktown was the obvious location for a chronicler of the river's sporting heritage and a public education resource. Bill McKinnon, a local businessman, provided the site, and the museum opened in 1983 with three galleries. An adjacent building housing an aquarium was completed two years later.

The museum exhibits the work of many famous fly tiers. Flies tied by Jack Atherton, Preston Jennings, Ira Gruber, Bert Miner, Everett Price, Charles DeFeo, Jack Storey, Jack Sullivan, and Wallace Doak are highlights of the collection. The astute visitor will be able to trace the development of many of the distinctive Miramichi patterns. Modern artists who create presentation patterns or recreate the classic feather-wing ties are represented by Ron Alcott and J. Martinez.

The efforts of the society have received international support. For example, Don Leyden of Brookfield, Connecticut has loaned or donated materials from his personal collection to enhance the displays. The walls of several galleries bear witness to the generosity of other donors with displays of prints by Henry McDaniel, Jack Atherton, Dick Leyden and others. The museum also recognizes important contributors to the Miramichi salmon tradition with a Hall of Fame.

One innovative way that the museum interacts with the community is the ecology school. Run every summer, the program accommodates children during the months of July and August and the families of visiting fishermen are welcome. In 1995 the museum, with the cooperation of the Irving Company, operated a week long conservation and salmon fishing school on the Cains for a group of native children. Isobel Loughead, the museum's manager, said, "The program was very successful and we hope to be able to repeat it. We'd like to run it for a month to increase the participation."

Wes Myles, a long-time salmon fishing acquaintance and a director of the museum, catalogued a few of latest additions to the collection for me. "We now have fly rods used by Father Elmer Smith and a beautiful diorama depicting the early native food fishery. But the most exciting development is the donation of an art and book collection from Donn Byrne of Sutter's Lodge which will establish our long awaited library." I certainly look forward to browsing the collection.

Central New Brunswick Woodmen's Museum

Few people in modern day North America, except for a few "extreme" sportspersons, have any experience with the degree of danger faced by the early woodmen of areas like the Miramichi. Jumping from log to log to free a jam, with the frigid spring-flood waters of the Miramichi eager to claim another victim, took both great courage and a less than developed concern for one's survival. The Woodmen's Museum in Boisetown guards the spirit of such men.

In addition to photographs and documents, the museum's exhibit hall features examples of the tools and transport of the early logging and trapping industries. Elsewhere on the grounds will be found recreations of a cookhouse and bunkhouse, a trapper's cabin, a blacksmith shop, a sawmill, and several other period buildings. Anyone interested in the history of working in the woods will find a visit more than rewarding.

Conclusion

William T. Griffin (1881-1974), who was primarily a hunter and hunting guide, wrote an abbreviated account of his life in *You're on the Miramichi*. He and his son Preston built and operated one of the early commercial lodges on the river, the Griff-Inn at Boisetown. A fitting conclusion to this *River Journal* is the last stanza from the Bill Griffin poem, "The Beautiful Miramichi."

From the birthplace of this river in the mountains of the west
To the tide that comes to meet it, Of all others it is best,
And God has used his talent in making such a stream
Where life is still worth living, and it is possible to dream,
Of Peace, and understanding, With love among mankind
Release from hell and torment, Humanity may find,
Pray when we cross the Jordan, and meet the Referee
We will hear the grand decision, You are on The Miramichi.

Other References

An excellent source of information concerning angling and hunting opportunities in New Brunswick is the Incredible Aim and Angle Adventures publication of Tourism New Brunswick, Dept. 337, P.O. Box 12345, Fredericton, NB E3B 5C3, or call (800) 561-0123.

A general tourist guide to the Miramichi region is available from the Miramichi Region Tourism Association, P.O. Box 264, Miramichi City, NB E1N 3A7.

Most of the works of Wayne and Herb Curtis are available from Goose Lane Editions, 469 King Street, Fredericton, NB E3B 1E5. *Fishing the Miramichi* by Wayne Curtis is available from New Ireland Press, 217 Aberdeen Street, Fredericton, NB E3B 1R6.

Evening upstream of the Priceville foot bridge.